T0132118

Me, Mom, and Dementia

Quinn Morris

AuthorHouse™
1663 Liberty Drive
Bloomington, IN 47403
www.authorhouse.com
Phone: 1 (800) 839-8640

© 2019 Quinn Morris. All rights reserved.
Credit to the artist: Sarah Louise Wilson

No part of this book may be reproduced, stored in a retrieval system,
or transmitted by any means without the written permission of the author.

Published by AuthorHouse 02/28/2019

ISBN: 978-1-5462-7900-6 (sc)
ISBN: 978-1-5462-7899-3 (e)

Library of Congress Control Number: 2019901424

Print information available on the last page.

This book is printed on acid-free paper.

Because of the dynamic nature of the Internet, any web addresses or links contained in this book may have changed
since publication and may no longer be valid. The views expressed in this work are solely those of the author and do not
necessarily reflect the views of the publisher, and the publisher hereby disclaims any responsibility for them.

authorHOUSE®

What is Dementia.

Dementia is a term that can involve many types of disabilities that resulting in memory decrease, the ability to think and reason and the ability for persons to care for themselves. For dementia to be considered, the symptoms must interfere with their daily life. These symptoms need to involve more than one category of brain function, such as memory, communication, judgment, or language. Different dementias have different symptoms, and progress in different ways.

Therefore, there can be several stages of dementia and according to the internet, one says there are three stages, another says there are five stages and still other says there are seven stages. The seven stages are:

1. No cognitive impairment – Unimpaired individuals experience no memory problems, and none are evident to a health care professional during a medical interview.
2. Very mild cognitive decline – Individuals at this stage feel as if they have memory lapses, especially in forgetting words or names of the location of keys, eyeglasses, or other everyday objects. But these problems are not evident during a medical examination or apparent to friends, family or co-workers.
3. Mild cognitive decline – Friends, family or co-workers notice deficiencies. Problems with memory or concentration may be measurable in clinical testing or discernible during a detailed interview. Common difficulties include:

    *   Word or name finding problems noticeable to family or close associates
    *   Decreased ability to remember names when introduced to new people
    *   Performance issues in social or work settings noticeable to family, friends, or co-workers
    *   Reading a passage and retaining material
    *   Losing or misplacing a valuable object
    *   Decline in ability to plan or organize.

4. Moderate cognitive decline – At this stage, a careful medical interview detects clear-cut deficiencies in the following areas:

- Decreased knowledge of recent occasions or current events
- Impaired ability to perform challenging mental arithmetic; for example, to count backward from 100 by 7s
- Decreased capacity to perform complex tasks, such as marketing, planning dinner for guests, or paying bills and managing finances
- Reduced memory of personal history
- The affected individual may seem subdued and withdrawn, especially in socially or mentally challenging situations.

5. Moderately severe cognitive decline – Major gaps in memory, and deficits in cognitive function emerge. Some assistance with day-to-day activities becomes essential. At this stage, individuals may:

- Be unable during a medical interview to recall such important details as their current address, their telephone number, the name of the college or high school from which they graduated
- Become confused about where they are, or about the date, day of the week, or season
- Have trouble with less challenging mental arithmetic; for example, counting backward from 40 by 4s or from 20 by 2s
- Need help choosing proper clothing for the season or the occasion
- Usually retain substantial knowledge about themselves and know their own name and the names of their spouse or children
- Usually require no assistance with eating or using the toilet

6. Severe cognitive decline – Memory difficulties continue to worsen, significant personality changes may emerge and affected individuals need extensive help with customary daily activities. At this stage, individuals may:

- Lose most awareness of recent experiences and events as well as of their surroundings
- Recollect their personal history imperfectly, although they generally recall their own name
- Occasionally forget the name of their spouse or primary care giver but generally can distinguish familiar from unfamiliar faces
- Need help getting dressed properly; without supervision, may make such errors as putting pajamas over daytime clothes or shoes on the wrong feet
- Experience disruption of their normal sleep/waking cycle
- Need help with handling details of toileting (flushing toilet, wiping and disposing of tissue properly)
- Have increasing episodes of urinary or fecal incontinence
- Experience significant personality changes and behavioral symptoms, including suspiciousness and delusions (for example, believing that their caregiver is an impostor); hallucinations (seeing or hearing things that are not really there); or compulsive, repetitive behaviors such as hand-wringing or tissue shredding
- Tend to wander and become lost

7. Very severe cognitive decline – This is the final stage of the disease when individuals lose the ability to respond to their environment, the ability to speak and ultimately, the ability to control movement.

- Frequently individuals lose their capacity for recognizable speech, although words or phrases may occasionally be uttered
- Individuals need help with eating and toileting and there is general incontinence of urine
- Individuals lose the ability to walk without assistance, then the ability to sit without support, the ability to smile, and the ability to hold their head up. Reflexes become abnormal and muscles grow rigid. Swallowing is impaired.

http://www.jim-mary.com/296945

This book is dedicated to my Mother, Elizabeth Lofton. She is the one who told me that I should sit down and write a book since I am constantly reading. I also am grateful to my husband for all his assistance while writing this book.

This book is also dedicated to Anita Siler, a close friend. She also edited some parts of the book for me and encouraged me to complete the project.

My Mom started showing signs of Dementia when she was about 96 years old. She would forget something and call herself stupid. "I am just so stupid," she said. Mom was aware of her memory lapses but felt like she was always doing stupid things. I would explain to her that everyone has moments of forgetfulness. I gave her an example of some of the times that I have forgotten some things, like where my keys were located. There were times when the she would forget the days of the week. We would get the newspaper every day because she liked to read them. She said that this was the way that she could keep up with what day it was.

Puzzles

Mom and I would work puzzles together. I would buy the large 300-piece puzzles with as much contrast as possible. When we worked together, she would find all the straight edges and I would put them together. I would add a few more parts of the puzzle and then she would finish it. She could sit hours, working on puzzles. She really enjoyed seeing the puzzle completed. One day when her great grandson was visiting, and they worked two puzzles together. She thought this was wonderful, because he was only five years old and he would tell her when she was putting the wrong piece in the wrong place.

When Mom got tired of working on a puzzle, she would get up and tell me to check and see how close she was to finishing it. Sometimes it would take her two to three days to finish a puzzle. As her dementia progressed, I would do more and more of the puzzle by myself and she would just watch me. When I asked her if she wanted to help, she would shake her head, "no." Later, the dementia got so bad that she would not even go toward the table if a puzzle was on it.

Reading

Mom loved to read. She had her own books in her room that she would read. They were catalogs, Christian books and the Bible. She would not read any other type of books. She also enjoyed reading her newspapers. She would understand everything that she read.

When Mom read the newspaper every day, she would always comment on what she read. She could tell you about every disaster that happened, every person that was killed, and how many people were on the obituary page. She would look at me and say that, "the world is coming to an end because the Bible says so." As her Dementia began to increase, she would get the paper and read just the first section of it. If she reads about a house break-in, she would ask if all the doors were lock and the windows were closed. Mom would not be satisfied until I would walk around the house and check every door and window in the house, sometimes she would do it herself. Mom would then check the door to her room, which does not have a lock on it and ask me why it doesn't lock. I would tell her that she did not need a lock on her bedroom door. When she would go to bed, she would block the door with boxes so that no one could get in. When I told her that that was not necessary, she would say that she knew that someone would try to get her on that night. When I explained about the alarm system, she would say that I was wrong, and she was right. If she read about a house fire, she would tell us to be careful because our house could catch on fire. She would then check the stove to be sure that we didn't leave it on. If she was looking at a catalog, she would talk about the pictures that she saw and show them to me, asking if a certain dress was pretty or a wig would look good on her. Sometimes she would find something in the catalog that she thought would look good on me and then she would say something funny and we would both laugh. Mom began to deteriorate more and more and soon she would not even pick up the paper.

Mom would sometimes, read her Bible until one or two o'clock in the morning. She would even quote scriptures from the Bible. She enjoyed reading the Old Testament. When she had trouble with some of the names, she would always ask me to pronounce them for her and there were some that I could not sound out. She would tease me by saying, "shame on you." As the Dementia progressed, Mom never stopped reading her Bible. She said that she wanted to read the entire Bible like she used to do, starting with Genesis and reading through to book of the Revelation. She would quote scriptures about prayer, and how the world was becoming more evil. One of her favorite sayings was, "God said that he was going to establish a new world with people that would obey him." She would talk a lot about the end of the world. She would say that she did not know what this world was coming too but unless the people change, this world would come to an end and very few people will live to see it. As her Dementia progressed, she would still get her Bible and read, but she would never go beyond the first three chapters of Genesis. Every time she picked up her Bible, Mom always started at the beginning of Genesis. It seemed that she could go no further. Later, she would read the first chapter of Genesis and nothing else.

Cooking

Mom loved to cook. When she came to live with us eleven years ago, she would cook all the meals for the family. She especially liked to cook cakes and pies. A meal was not a dinner without desert. As her dementia was diagnosed, she became a little absent minded. She would start cooking something and forget that she had left it on the stove. There were times when we would cook together, and she would tell me that I did not know what I was doing. When I would cook by myself, she would always ask what I was cooking. If she did not think I was doing it right, she would say, "You don't know what you are doing." If I was following a recipe, I would tell her that I was using a recipe and then show it to her. She would then say that the recipe was wrong. I would just say okay mom and continue with the meal. When the food was cooking mom would sometimes look in the pots and ask me what I was cooking. She would then make a face as if it was something that she did not want.

I did not realize that she was losing some taste sensations. After a while there was very little food that she seemed to like except for desserts. Even her favorite foods that I cooked, were no longer wanted. When I cooked, what I called, "goulash", a mixture of many textures of food, she would say that it was delicious. Yet, when I would cook it again at another time, she would say that I could not cook. She always had to have desert with her dinners and she preferred cake or cookies. I would buy these because I did not want to cook them. Mom would tell me that she would cook t hem herself. I bought cake mix and pie crush so that she could cook either of them. She cooked an apple pie and she thought it was delicious, but no one could eat it but her. Later in her Dementia, Mom would take the food from her plate and mix everything together, usually in a glass, eat some of it and cover the rest with a napkin or a paper towel. Mom would mix greens, cornbread, cake, corn, and orange juice together, take one spoon full or eggs, bacon, toast, jam and Ensure, cover it with a napkin, telling us not to touch it. She would tell us not to touch it because she was going to eat it later, which she never did. I would make sure that she would drink at least one Ensure a day and that there was always snack food that she could eat during the day. She enjoyed oranges, pears, and bananas and would eat them during the day. As the Dementia progressed, she would take the orange, peel it, eat one or two pieces of it and wrap it in a napkin, telling us not to touch it. She would do the same thing with a pear and/or a banana. She would never completely eat any of it.

As she was beginning to deteriorate more, she always thought that she did the cooking. Every now and then she would think that she was cooking. She would check the stove to see if she left something on it cooking. She could be watching television and would ask if she left beans on the stove cooking or bread in the oven. When told no, she would have to check it out for herself. She would check the stove more than once because she kept forgetting and sometimes, she would say that her food was burning and ask me to check it for her.

Bathing

Mom was determined not to smell bad. She believed in bathing, putting on clean clothes, and washing her hair. If she felt like she was not clean, she would say that she was stinking. During the last five years of her life, we had a home care person come to our home twice a week to give Mom a bath. She was very particular about who gave her a bath. If her regular person was not able to come, she would try to give herself a bath. During the other days of the week, she would give herself a sponge bath. When her Dementia began to progress, I would help her bathe. She told me that I did not bathe her like the home care person did. All I could do was smile.

Clothing

In the beginning, mom loved to go to church, go shopping, go to restaurants, and over to my business partner's house. She would choose her own clothing but sometimes get her seasons mixed. During the cooler weather, she would wear her light-weight clothing and during the warmer weather, she would choose her heavier clothing. I could not tell her differently even when she would go outside. When it was cooler, she would tell me to get her a coat because she was cold. I had already told her how cold it was but she did not believe me. She had to find out for herself. She made sure she was dressed up for church, wearing one of her favorite hats. She only had six hats, but she would wear only two of them. Her shoes were a different issue. She would wear the right color shoes with every outfit at first. When she chose a pair of shoes that did not match her outfit and I would suggest that she wear another pair, she would let me know that I did not know what I was talking about. Later in her life, she would choose the shoes that were comfortable on her feet because they would swell. She also had arthritis in her feet and would choose the shoes that was most comfortable.

Hair

Mom was always complaining about her hair. She did not want to go natural. At first, my sister and/or sister-in-law would give her a permanent. When they could no longer do it, I would get a beautician to come to the house. She only wanted her hair pressed straight with no curls because she felt that she could do it herself. I found a beautician that I thought she would like to press her hair. She told the beautician that she wanted her hair pressed with a straighten comb. She did not want anyone to use the flat iron because she did not believe that it would work. The beautician was very patient with mom, doing exactly what she was told, using the hair oil mom took with her and not putting any curls in her hair. Her hair was pressed straight but mom did not think it was straight enough. Even though mom complained, she went back to the same beautician on several occasions. The last time she went, she scared the beautician because she had chest pains. She took her nitro and the pain was relieved. Mom decided that she wanted to have a press and curls this time. The beautician did a beautiful job, but mom wet hair and the curls were gone. She blamed it on the beautician.

Temperature

At home, mom was always cold. She would put on a slip, a T-shirt, a dress, and a sweater. Sometimes she would wear a night jacket along with everything else. The temperature in the house would be seventy-four degrees, but she would still be cold. When the temperature was hot outside, she always wanted the air conditioner on inside, but she would always dress the same. On the other hand, the house would be hot, and she would need a blanket because she was cold, or she would be hot when the house was cold. I never did understand this.

Cane

Mom walked with a cane. She had three of them, but she preferred to only use her favorite one which was very colorful. She also had several walkers and a wheelchair. She would use her cane whenever she went to places such as church, shopping, the doctor's office, beauty salon, and the dentist office. As her Dementia got worst, her knees would give out on her, her feet would hurt and sometimes she would fall. She had never fallen while outdoors, although she had tripped on several occasions. She would take a missed step but as long as she had her cane, she did not fall. There were a couple of times when she walked without her cane and fell. She had fallen about eight times indoors. She never hurt herself and was always able to pull herself up except for the last time when she called me for help. With my help, she was able to get on her feet. She then told me that the Lord would not let her fall and get hurt. You see, she had enough faith to believe that the Lord was with her, even in her falls and God would protect her.

Mom did not like the wheelchair or the walkers. She tried to use the walker on one occasion but decided that it was not safe, so she refused to use it. This was the same with the wheelchair. She would feel weak in her legs and when asked if she wanted the wheelchair, she would say that she did not need it. As she became weaker, we would always take the wheelchair with us. One day when we went grocery shopping, she decided that she did not need her wheelchair. I tried to convince her that the store was very large, and she would get tired from walking around looking for the items that she wanted. When we got to the store she started shopping and within ten minutes mom was so tired that she could not go any further. I was glad that I had brought the wheelchair with us, and when she sat down, she sighed and gave me a smile. She never told me "thank you" but I knew that she appreciated the chair.

Another time, she decided to walk home. She always thought that her home was within walking distance. One day she was adamant that she was going home and that I could not stop her. She kept going to the door trying to get out, which she could not do because I had a child guard on the knob. It was even hard for me sometimes to open the door, so I knew that she would not be able to open it. On this day, she insisted that I did not know what I was talking about and she was going home. When asked how she would get there, she said that she would catch a bus.

I told her that there were no buses close to the house. When I was younger, she never learned to drive so she would take public transportation wherever she went. In St. Louis, Missouri, the public transportation was very good, and she would catch the bus when and wherever she wanted to go. I opened the door for her and I watched to see where she would go. She had her favorite cane with her. She would usually walk to the end of the driveway and turn around. This time, she walked a little further. I just watched because I did not think that she would go very far. She walked to the end of the block and I noticed that she was slowing down. I did not have her wheelchair out, so the neighbor watched her while I went into the house to get her chair. When I caught up with her, she was happy and ready to sit down. She told me that she was tired. When she got back to the house, she rested for a while and decided it was time for her to go home. She tried opening the front and back doors but could not get them opened. She kept saying, "Let me out!" and She never walked that far again.

Church

Mom loved to go to church. She was determined to go to church for every service. Our services were on Sunday morning and Wednesday night. Sometimes she would not eat dinner because she wanted to be ready to go to church on time. She believed that if she would eat before church, she would not be able to enjoy the services because she would have to use the restroom during the services. When she got to church she would sing her song. She always had a songbook with her and the she would sing the old hymnals. When she would finish her song, she would ask me why I did not help with the song. I told her that she and I did not sing songs the same way. She would say that she knew how the song went and I did not know what I was talking about. Sometimes I would argue with her and I would sing a small portion of the song like I knew it should be sung. She would look at me and say that she was right, and I was wrong. I would agree with her because, believe it or not, we were in church while she was talking.

When she was not allowed to sing, she would wonder why. She wanted to know what the reason that she could not sing. I would explain to her that she decided to sing at the wrong time and/or she did not indicate that she had a song that she was ready to sing. Sometimes she was asked if she wanted to sing and she would say no because she had forgotten her hymnal.

Mom would sit in her room and practice the songs so that she could choose the one that she planned to sing when she got to church that night. She would always ask me if I knew the song that she was going to sing, and I learned to yes or no. If I said no, she would say "I know you know the words to this song." I would let her sing it to me and I would shake my head to indicate that I really did not know the song. If I did know the words to the song, I would let her know that her tune was not my tune. She would again let me know that I did not know what I was talking about and continued singing her song.

Mom enjoyed talking to the members at the church and enjoyed the way they would greet her. She was the oldest member of the church and was really appreciated. There was another senior member that she enjoyed sitting next to. When mom was not able to make it to every service, this senior member would always ask about her. When this senior member did not attend, mom would ask about her. As she began to deteriorate, she would forget the names of some of the members that were in her circle.

Mom enjoyed going to Bible study classes. She would study her lessons and make comments on the lesson and/or answer questions. As she declined, she would sometimes talk out of turn, but the church members understood and would let her talk. This was really appreciated by me. Afterward, she would just sit and listen.

We went to a small church and mom was very concern about the growth of the church. She would talk about what her Pastor husband used to do to grow the church and wonder why her current pastor was not doing it. She would call him a youngster and tell him about his clothing which she thought were too big. One time, she told him to pull up his pants because they were too big and too long. He did what she told him to do. She was always aware of what was happening in church.

Prayer

Mom was a praying woman. At home, she would be in her room praying and praising the Lord. She would do these two to three times a day. When she could, she would get down on her knees to pray. But as she began to decline, she would sit in her chair and pray. She would pray for her children, the church members, her siblings, and her friends. She would also pray for President Obama and the problems of this world, as she saw them.

When she went to church for prayer, she would always comment on the number of people who attended prayer, which was very few. She also wondered why the pastor was not in the prayer service. Again, she was comparing him to her husband who was always in prayer and would, in many cases, lead the prayer. He would be in Prayer and Bible Band listening to the women who were present. He would call for prayer and he would be there to start it off. During the regular service times, he would be sure to be in prayer with the other members of the church.

Humor vs Frustration

The television:

Mom enjoyed watching television. She liked the old sitcoms, news, and religious programs. As the dementia progressed, mom did not watch television very much, but when she did, she enjoyed watching "The Golden Girls." Later, she felt that the people on the television were looking at her and/or talking to her. She would ask me if they could see her. I tried to explain to her that they could not see her. I gave her the example of a picture. I asked her if the person in the picture was looking at her and she would say "no." She would not believe that the people on the television was not looking her or talking to her. One day she became very upset because she felt that the person on the television was looking at her and she tried to prove it by moving slightly to one side and believing that the person on the television was following her with their eyes. She would say "Stop looking at me."

One day, the commentator was talking about getting interviews for a job. She got up from the chair, went to stand in front of the television, and started talking back to the television. I told her that they could not hear her, but she was adamant that they could. She kept talking to the television on several occasions. One day, while talking to the television, she had a conversation with the commentator, where she kept saying "huh", "I can't hear you", "what did you say?", "okay," and "you don't know what you are talking about".

We had to stop looking at westerns and some of the news that showed a lot of violence. If there was a burning house, she would think that our house was going to catch fire. If there was a western picture on with guns shooting, she would be afraid that a person would walk in on us with a gun. One day there were two women talking to each on the television and she stood in front of the television and joined in on the conversation. She kept asking them if they were talking to her. As the women continued their conversation, she walked closer to the television, still asking if they were talking to her. When the women finished their conversation, she would return to her chair and sit down, apparently satisfied that the conversation was over.

The dolls:

I have many dolls of all kinds in my house, both large and small. When we moved to Texas, she decided that she wanted some dolls in her room. I ordered them for her from many of the catalogs that she had gotten. She chose a girl and boy doll. The boy was dressed as a fireman and the girl was dressed very dainty with a teddy bear. She placed them on a small chest at the foot of her bed. As she began to deteriorate, she would cover them with a small blanket or one of her jackets because she thought they were getting cold. She also said that they would follow her with their eyes. At night, they were not sleeping like they should, so she would cover their heads so that the night light would not bother them.

One day, I caught her talking to one of the eighteen inches doll I have in one of my cabinets. This doll is dressed as a little old lady. She walked toward the cabinet and asked the doll what she was doing. I asked her who she was talking to and she told me that she needed to talk to the lady. When I asked her what lady, she looked at me and told me that I saw the lady. Again, I asked her what lady, and she would say, "Don't be stupid." You see that lady standing right there (pointing at the doll.)" She turned her back on me and began to introduce herself to the doll. She did not wait for the doll to say anything, she kept talking. After she had said what she wanted to say, she would stop talking as if she was waiting for the doll to say something. If the doll did not say anything, she would start talking again. Again, she would stop talking, waiting for the doll to say something. If she did not get an answer, she just shrugged her shoulders and return to her favorite chair and sat down. After she sat down, she would look at all the dolls and wonder why they were looking at her. She would ask me on a regular basis if the dolls were following her with their eyes. After I told her "no", she would say that they really looked like it. Sometimes, she would move from place to place, looking at the dolls eyes to see if they were looking at her. She was always positive that the doll's eyes were moving whenever she moved.

During her last days, she would always check the dolls to see if they were sleeping. Before she went to bed, she would ask me where the children were and if they were in their beds sleeping. Sometimes, she would walk around the room making sure that they were sleeping. When she was satisfied that everyone was sleeping, she would go to bed and sleep. At other times, she would say that she heard the children, but I would assure her that the children had gone home and therefore she did not hear them. At other times, she would look under her bed because the children were supposed to be playing there or they were standing around her bed, talking to her. My dolls were the children that she was talking about.

My House:

I live in a one-story house, with my library, which consist on only one room, on the second floor. Mom's rooms were located on the first floor closest to the kitchen and family room. She had her own television, but she preferred to watch it with the family. Either I or my husband would sit with her while she watched television. She enjoyed watching religious programs. Old movies such as 'I love Lucy', 'The Golden Girls', 'Hallmark', and some cowboy movies.

As she began to deteriorate, she would forget where her room was. In the beginning, she would get upset with herself and call herself stupid. Sometimes, she would laugh about it, look at me and ask," Which way should I go?" I would only have to point, and she would say "I don't know why I am always getting so tangled up." There were times when she would walk around the whole house looking for her bathroom which was connected to her bedroom. She felt that our house was just too big. When she finally came back to where she stared from, I asked her where she was going. She told me that she was trying to find her bathroom. All to do was point and she would finally make it to the restroom. She looked at me and say, "I always get turned around."

There were times when mom would walk around the house and come back to where I was and ask who owned the house. I would tell her that I owned the house. She would then ask who owns the other half of the house. I would tell her that I own the whole house. Then she would ask me who were my neighbors and where did they live. I told her that my neighbors have their own house and they lived in those houses. When she wants to know the names of our neighbors, I would tell her who they are. She would then ask what color they were. After I tell her they are White, and she would say that they own my house. I would try to explain to her that they own their own homes and I pay the mortgage on this house that we were living in. She told me that I was wrong because according to her, I could not afford to pay for this house. She would sit for a while and then point tried toward her room and ask who lives there. I tried to explain that that was her room and it is a part of my house. She let me know that I am not right because the house it was too big for one family. I tried to explain to her that this is one house, my house with several rooms, and I pay for it. We have gone through this on several occasions, ending with the cost of the house.

As I said before, my house is on one level. When she would get ready to go to her room, she would go to the door and look back at me and say, "Is this my room?" I would tell her yes and she would ask me if I was sure. I would tell her yes again and she was satisfied. There have also been times when she would say that I should go downstairs to get something for her. I would let her know that there is no downstairs.

Her Room:

Mom would keep her room clean. She had quite a lot of things in her room and in the beginning, she knew where everything was. As she began to deteriorate more, she would rearrange things such as clothing, linen and hair products. When it came time to find an item, she would not be able to remember where she put it. This would frustrate her to no end. She would go through her closet and chest drawers, pulling every item out until she found what she was looking for. If she could not find it, she would become very frustrated and call me to help her look. There were times when she would not find what she was looking for and would become more frustrated. She would then call on me to help her look for what she had lost, and I would become frustrated. Then I would help her put things back where they belong, but she would let me know that I was putting them wrong place. When I would leave the room, she would place the items where she wanted them so when I would look for them, I would not be able to find them.

She would never leave her rooms messy. According to Mom, she had to put the items where she could find them, but when it came time for her to use them, of course, she could not find them. When I did find what she was looking for, she would ask where I found them and then wonder how they got there because according to her, she did not put them there. When I asked her who put them there, she would smile sometimes, and other times would become more frustrated. She would be so frustrated that she would again call herself "stupid." As she becomes more and more forgetful, she would misplace more and more items, but she would always clean up whatever she messed up.

Her Money:

Mom had her own checking and savings account when she first moved in with us. Then she decided that she wanted another signature on her accounts so that she could better keep up with them. My husband's name was on her checking account and she called him her secretary so that when she wanted to buy something, he would write the check out for her and she would sign it. I was put on her savings account. Mom loved looking at catalogs and she liked to pick out things that she wanted. On holidays, she would make sure that a present was sent to all her children for their family. She was able to buy anything that she wanted. Her main concern was that she would have enough money to bury herself. Dad was from the old school. He had small insurances policies for her and larger ones for himself.

As Mom got older, she kept worrying about her funeral expenses. We had a pre-burial plan for her and would let her know that everything was being taken care of. We would show her the bills so that she could sign the checks. She was always aware of how much money she had in her bank accounts because she was given all the statements that came into the mail.

Mom was generous with her money. She used it to help her children and grandchildren and was not repaid by any of them. She would pay her tithes every month as well as give a free-freewill offering. If she saw someone in need and knew that she could help, she would do so. The senior mothers at the church would get a present from every Mother's Day and Christmas day. The children at church would get presents from her at Christmas and Easter.

Later in her life, she began to misplace her money, calling herself hiding it from my husband and different people in her imagination. When she could not find it, she would accuse someone in the house of stealing it. She would pick on my husband, saying that he would go into her room and steal her money. Sometimes, she would pull me aside and say, "I don't want to hurt your feelings, but your husband is stealing my money. I would tell her that it was not true and would go into her room and look for the money. Sometimes I would find it and sometimes not. It got so bad, that my husband refused to go into her room because it really frustrated her. Even when he was asked to get something for her, he would not do so. Every time she would ask him, he would look at me and I would know that he was not going into her room. These accusations were transferred to any man who came into our house. When my sister and her husband came to visit, she would watch him closely to make sure that he did not go into her room. I told him that it was best not to go into her room, or she would accuse him of taking her money.

When my mother hid her money, she would forget where she put it. She would search and search and then become frustrated when she could not find it and call herself stupid. I would look for it and sometimes finding it and sometimes not finding it. I would give her the money she said that she lost. One time, she misplaced $80.00 and I could never find it. She kept insisting that my husband had taken it. When I told her that he does not go into her room any more, she did not believe me. She did not believe it. She said that he had gone into her purse and taken it. She was adamant that he had taken it. I decided to give her a portion of the money, letting her think that I found it and I would be keeping it for her. She agreed to this arrangement. We never did find it. I think, she could have flushed it down the toilet because she would put her money in the pockets of her dresses. There were times when I washed her clothes, I would find her money. I would give it to her. She would agree, but every now and then she would ask me how much money that I was keeping for her. She was content with me keeping her money because she knew that I would give it to her whenever she wanted it.

Going Home:

As her dementia worsen, she decided that it was time for her to go home. The house that she had lived in for the past eleven years, was no longer where she lived. She got her suitcase that she keeps under her bed and started packing her clothes. When her suitcase was full, she would get boxes and bags and fill them up. She always collected boxes and plastic bags in her room. Every now and then, I would take some of them out because they were too much junk. She would take all her clothes out of her closet and put them on a chair in the kitchen, asking me when I was going to take her home. I would tell her that she is already home. She would say that this is not her home. I would ask her where her home was. She would say that I knew where she lived, and I should not treat her like she was stupid. When she was not looking, I would take the clothes and put them back in her closet.

One time later, she decided it was time for her to go home, she packed her clothes and decided to clean out her closet again. When she could not find enough boxes or bags, she would just put them in the kitchen on the chairs. This time, when she took her clothes out of the closet, she told me that they were not her clothes and I could give them away. I tried to explain to her that they were her clothes and that she still needed them. She became frustrated and said that they were not her clothes and would not let me put them back in her closet. She picked up her suitcase, sweaters and cane and she said that she was ready to leave. I had to wait two days before I could put them back in the closet. As she deteriorated more, decided that nothing in her room belonged to her. It was not even her room and she needed to go home. She needed some clean clothes, cook some food for her husband, and wash her clothes. She also felt that her husband would be angry with her if she did not get home. She did not want her husband to be mad at her. I told her she was home, and she would ask me if I was telling her the truth.

Her Relatives:

Mom believed that some of her aunts were in walking distance from the house. She kept saying that she could walk to their house because if was around the corner and only a block away. She wanted to walk out the door and find their house. We had to watch her because she would open the door and go for a walk. At first, she would not go very far because she said that she was tired. Many times, she would walk outside without her cane and we would be afraid that she would fall. She had fallen several times in the house and did not break any bones.

One day when my husband and I had to go someplace, we asked my brother to sit with his mother. When we came home, my brother told me that my mother had tried to leave the house and he not let her open the front door. She picked up her cane and hit him across the head. She did not hurt him, but she was upset because she had not seen him in several weeks. After this incident, we decided to put a child lock on the door that she could not open.

One night she decided that she wanted to again go and see the relative that she thought lived around the corner from our house. It was dark outside. I tried to tell her that it was too dark to walk outside. She did not believe me and kept trying to get out of the door. I opened the door to show her. The first time she accepted the fact that it was too dark. Another time, I opened the door and she decided to walk out. When she saw that there were no street lights, she turned around and came back into the house. She sat down and asked me to drive her to see her relatives. I told her that they were in Tennessee or dead. She asked where she was when he died. She did not believe me.

There were times when she and I would sit together, and she would ask me about some of her relatives and she would name a few. When I told her that they were dead, she would say they were not. She asked me about my dad. I told her that he was dead and that he had died in 2002. I told her that she had attended his funeral. She said that she was not there. She would then call out the names of several of her aunts and uncles. All I had to say was that they were dead. She said that she did not believe me, and they could not all be dead. I told her that they were older than she was, and she was 98. She then called me stupid.

Sleep:

In the beginning, mom would take a nap during the day and sleep through the night. Later, she began to get her days and nights mixed up. She would take naps during the night and sleep during the day. I could never keep her awake during the day; I would call her name or touch her, and she would wake up and say, "I'm not sleep," and before you know it, she was snoring softly again. When the dementia worsen, she would be awake days and mostly through the nights. The doctor gave her sleeping pills and anxiety pills, but she would still sleep about four hours during the night and get up and walk through the house. She would be dressed in her night gown, slippers, house coat, and turn on all the lights in the house. She would come into my room and wake me up. She wanted something to eat and she was ready to go home. I would get up and give her something to eat and then sit with her because she was not ready to go back to bed. If I was tired, I would turn off the lights, indicating that it was time to go back to bed. On several nights, I stayed up all night with her.

Crime:

Mom was always afraid that someone would break into the house. She would say that she heard someone knocking on her window and or knocking on her door. I would reassure her that the alarm was on and if someone came in, the alarm would go off. I would show her that the outside doors were locked but that was not enough for her. She would go into her room, lock her bathroom door and put things in front of her bedroom door so that no one could get in to get her. I would ask her to stop blocking the door. I would have to say it several times before she would let me in. When I left the room, she would put the stuff against the door again so that she could feel safe.

Forgetfulness:

We would sit and talk about general things such as the news, politics, etc. She would start out on topic and then start rambling about the neighbors that supposedly occupied part of my house. This is a one family house. Who were they? Where were they? How much do they pay to stay here? She just could not believe that we were the only family living in this house. I told her that we were the only ones living in my house. She would then go back to our original conversation.

Then she would say that my house was not her house and that she did not live here. She used to live in Hayti and St. Louis. She believed that she could walk from my house in Texas and find the house that she used to live in. I would tell her that it was too far for her to walk there, and she would let me know that she would catch a bus. She wanted to know if she could call them so that they could come and pick her up and take her home. I told her that there were no buses running in the area in which I live. After a while, she would accept what I told her.

She then decided that she would call her relatives. She found the yellow pages of the telephone book, starting at the beginning, looking for the telephone number of her relatives who she claimed lived around the corner. I would let her look through the book for a while. When she could not what she was looking for, she became frustrated. She would continue to ask me about them and I would tell her the same thing, repeatedly, they are dead. She would ask when they died and would tell her many years ago and she would let me know that she did not believe me, again. Mom would ask me if I was telling the truth. This happened many times.

Mom would open the door and look out. Sometimes she would walk to the end of the drive way and turn around. One day she decided to go further down the street and forgot where she was, so, we had to put child guards on the door knobs. She would try to open the doors but when she could not do so, she would ask my husband or myself to let her out. I would open the door sometimes and watch to see where she was going. She would go a little way and turn around again. I would go to the end of the drive way so that she could see me when she turns around to come back. Most of the time, she had her cane with her.

Summary:

When Mom reached the age of ninety-five, she was beginning to deteriorate more and more each year. When she reached the age of ninety-eight birthday in October, her condition rapidly declined. During this decline, my focus was not on my feelings; my main concern was my mother and how she felt about slowly losing her memory. In the beginning, she was aware that she was having trouble remembering; at first, she would make fun of it. She had a good sense of humor. But the more she deteriorated, the more frustrated she became and the more she struggled. During simple things like bathing herself, making her bed and reading became challenging. Seeing her struggle with these simple tasks was difficult, and I felt helpless and sad. I knew that there was nothing that I could do but pray.

During her times of lucidity, I encouraged her, talked with her, and prayed with her. Even though our roles changed, and I was now her caregiver, I never for got that she was still mother. She was the parent, and it was my job as her daughter to encourage her to continue to do as much for herself as she could. I wanted her to feel independent. You see, I believed that since she ha taken care of me, it was time for me to take care of her, like a daughter should. So, I would never tell her that what she was doing something was wrong when she was trying to do something right. I remember when she put her dress on inside out. Since weren't leaving the house, I did not try to change it because she was very content with the way it was.

As Mom's health declined further, she would talk about her life and relive incidents from her youth. She remembered the names of some of her relatives who had long-since passed away. In fact, one day when she wanted to talk to her long-lost cousin Rebecca, I would not give her the telephone number because it was not available. When I told her that Rebecca was dead and explained why she would not find her name in a Texas directory, she told me that I did not know what I was talking about.

Sometimes I would stay up all night watching her because she refused to get in bed and go to sleep. For some reason, at nighttime, she needed to turn on the lights, so she could see. She would also come into my bedroom looking for thins that she had misplaced, all the while calling my name. One night she decided that she wanted to go outdoors, and she could not find the door, so she started banging on the windows, messing up my blinds, yelling, "Let me

Out! Let me Out!" She went from window to window. I was afraid for her, so I stood back and watched because I did not want her to hurt herself.

This time was exhausting for me, and I frequently became upset. Many times, I felt like screaming at her, but I restrained myself. I figured that when she found out she couldn't leave, she would settle down. It took her fifteen minutes to realize that she could not get out through the windows. In the morning she did not remember what she had done even when I reminded her of it. Sometimes, she would tell me that I did not know what I was talking about. I learned early on not to argue with her in those cases, because I would never win.

Before her health declined, Mom loved to cook. She would do all the cooking for the family because she thought I didn't know how to cook. And when I did cook, she would eat but always stated that she could do better. I had to limit her cooking time because she would leave the stove on or burn the food. I also kept my knives dull because I did not want her to cut herself. When she tried to clean up after she finished eating, sometimes forgot to turn the water off. She caused flooding in the kitchen and the bathroom. When she could help with the chores, she felt valued.

Although my mother's dementia was difficult for her and for me, my mother taught me many things during this time. She continued to pray, read her bible, and sing. When things got tough for her, she would always whisper a prayer. She would praise God for the little things.

Don't get me wrong, there were times when I became very frustrated or angry because I could do nothing about her illness. At times, I wanted to give up and place her in an assisted living facility. But I remembered the promise we, the family, made to our dad on his deathbed: to care for Mom and never place her in a nursing home. That was a promise I was determined to keep if I could.

Mom's illness also taught me patience. For years I prayed to God for patience, and the God-given patience helped me deal with my mother's illness. There were times when I had to go into my bathroom and cry to avoid raising my voice to her. Deep inside, I wanted to just scream. Instead, God gave me a song to sing, and I would find peace through song. God is a good God, and through His goodness, I was able to take some of the verbal abuse from my mother.

Another thing my mother taught me throughout her life was to be faithful to God. That meant going to church, working in the church, reading the Bible, paying my tithes, giving my offerings, praising God, and meeting Him in prayer. It did not matter how she felt; when it came time for church, she never missed an opportunity to attend. Sometimes she would be ready before I was, and other times I had to wait for her. One Sunday, she was not doing well, but she wanted to go to church so I helped her get dressed. At that point, it was necessary for her to use her wheelchair, but she didn't like it, especially when she went into a church building. But since she needed to go, she accepted the chair and had a good time once we were there.

I know that I am a better person for taking care of my mother. Because of her, I am at peace with myself, and I really feel good about the way I took care of her. I thought I had peace before, but now I am more tolerant of others. I know how to let more things go. I know my limitations. I know when to listen, when to speak, when to confront, and when to back down. I also learned that I did not know as much about myself as I thought I did.

I thank God for my mother and for everything she taught me during her illness. It strengthened my resolve in the Lord and increased my understanding of what people go through when dealing with their illnesses, mentally, physically, and spiritually. Every day, I thank God for my mother. I miss her, and I think about her often. She encouraged me to take some time for myself, and now, I am.

My prayer: Lord, I thank you for giving me the strength to take one day at a time. Look on thecaregivers and give them the strength to make it on a daily basis. Help them to realize that they are doing a special service for you Amen.

Printed in the United States
By Bookmasters